AN AVIARY OF COMMON BIRDS

Lalah-Simone Springer is a poet and speculative fiction writer from Dagenham, Essex (she/they). In 2021, an early manuscript of *An Aviary of Common Birds* was long-listed for the #Merky New Writers Prize and they received the Community Engagement Artist Grant - for artists that reimagine our shared spaces and stimulate social engagement, creative expression and collective empowerment. Previous collaborations as a performance artist have been staged at The Barbican, Whitechapel Gallery, Folkstone Fringe and Almanac Project Space.

Cyclical Music

A selection of these poems were first written in response to music produced by Curtis Elvidge, which became the collaborative project and album Cyclical Music. The spoken word x electronic jazz project explores themes of liminal spaces through the lens of romantic relationships, suggesting that liminal spaces are a place for 'becoming'.

Listen to the album in full on Spotify or Bandcamp.

Tracklist
1. At the Strikers
2. April Showers
3. Secret Argent
4. Rupture
5. Repair
6. He Remembers with a Smile...
7. Sleep-
8. -wake

Credits
Words by Lalah-Simone Springer, music by Curtis Elvidge.
Drums on 'At the Strikers' and 'Rupture' by Benoit Parmentier.
Marimba on 'Rupture' by Benny Clark.
Vocals on 'Sleep-Wake' by Liz Gre.

Recorded and mixed at the Premises Studio A by Curtis Elvidge.
Mastered by Cicely Balston at Air Studios.
Album cover art by Joe Gamble.

An Aviary of Common Birds

Lalah-Simone Springer

Broken Sleep Books

ISBN: 978-1-915760-30-2

Cover designed by Aaron Kent

Edited & Typeset by Aaron Kent

Broken Sleep Books Ltd
Rhydwen
Talgarreg
Ceredigion
SA44 4HB

Broken Sleep Books Ltd
Fair View
St Georges Road
Cornwall
PL26 7YH

For the gal dem

Contents

Part 1

Part 2

Part 1

There is so much becoming to be done.

The cries of other people's children echo through window, off tile, to rouse your aching breast.
Days pass, afternoon sun seeps into the pool of still warm water at your feet.

Wait.
Wait.
Wait.

You'd rung yourself out waiting for the one or two, but they were mind and body, here all along.
It's all very well being woke, but you'd only opened two eyes.

You don't have to know the universe, you are the universe.
You don't have to run when it hurts to crawl. You don't have to know everything.
You don't have to know everything.

There's nothing wrong with you.

Opening is so often breaking. Softening is so often hard.
Mending hurts, draws focus like the itch of a scab. Try not to pick at yourself

Tip your toes past the confines of eggshell perfection, past safety and solidity, into roots.
The space between is sacred - those who live there know. The space between is elemental, formless essence. (Formless, shapeless, endless)

Who knows how long, who knows how low
How deep the crevasse, how sharp the slope.

There is so much becoming to be done.

The cries of other people's children echo through window, off tile, to rouse your aching breast.

Days pass, moonlight shifts over the pool of still warm water at your feet, over the tension of your knee, over your worn hips, over your tense shoulders, your taut jaw.

There's nothing wrong with you.

Wait.
Wait.
Wait.

Six Months

He leans against the iron railing,
chipped tooth gleaming down at
a woman passing with her dog

when I feel myself reflected:
Canal water shimmers, framing the fuss of fish
held at bay.
Starlings soar tethered to the sky by
lines of joy.
Between all this the faces skitter, circling.

I find him seconds later
after my haze fills with letters
(as it always does)
hoisting his jeans, running
past the slowly encroaching, curious crows

a face in a crowd, unnamed.

Dasheen

Tuesday: a mountain of rice, one roast potato, two pieces of fried fish with bones and skin softened through oil, draped in sour rings of pepper and onion, home made coleslaw, tea.

The plate is piled high and hot before you even take off your shoes:
you may not wash up plates,
you may not serve them first.
This is how my grandparents show their love.

Nanny's lips purse while she spoons mounds of rice-and-peas onto the plate
Her studied silence except to ask: 'Is this enough?'

I never want as much as she tries to give me.
I make myself small in the face of their love,
I do not know how to ask for more.
All these things are true at once.

Thursday: chalky boiled yam, dasheen, potato. Wilted lettuce and fresh sliced white onion, tinned tuna with hot pepper sauce, salad cream, white pepper, salt. And tea.

"How much you want Sam?"

They stand over his plate together,
Her metal spoon sings as it scrapes mash from the cast-iron pot.
Her soft black woolly hat meets his thinning salt and pepper pate as they look down.

After 50 years together, they do not always need to say thank you.
Sometimes their outlines blur together.

Sunday: Roast chicken, roast potatoes, rice-and-peas, macaroni cheese, salad, home made coleslaw, mixed vegetables, hard food.

We crowd around the brightly covered table on Boxing Day, we 30.
We jostle, slipping plantain into aunties plate, stealing chicken skin and slopping gravy,
but we fill up the young ones first.

Their plates are piled high and hot - may they never need to ask.

How to Pronounce Dagenham

For Jodie Chesney

First relax ur froat, ur maaf, ur vibe
Not much to do about not much to do so ya chat shit:
Wiv ya white shirt unbuttoned over West Ham strip
Clanging pawnshop platinum on a baby blackbird's chest.
Narmy Army swells over Heathway, trailing broken Dagz like
'U wot mate?' Fist tatts, clapbacks, my brother's best mate got...

                                        that C2C tracks constant clanging
                            in her veins, she got a lulled goodbye to Percy, to the pawnshop
                                        goodbye to Jo: sun glows platinum
                                        through her, straight to the grass on
                            which she sits. not much to do about not much to do, a
                            purple bracelet twirls, lip corners curl when he calls her 'baby'
                                        soft as sweet tarmac, watching blackbirds
                            crows? crows watch back. breath rises, settles, in her chest

Which flowers in Foxglove, which blossoms in Columbine:
She gavvers em. Playgrand wood chips skitter to soften the earf on which she
sits.
Not
much
to
do
about
Not
much
to
do,
a

15

The Ballad of Roz & Victoria (Wifed Up)

U-haul lesbo?
Nah, mate.
I wanna be
spreadin' my seed
Sun out, guns out
Crescent scars
Brand new nips
Looking fit as fuck.
Didn't mean t'
get locked down -
can't resist a posh girl.

She's in a screamo band.

Spent six hours on Skype
last night, light playing
across her pixelated tits
Fuuuck, me!
She sees me as I am.
She sees me as a man.
I want to hold her and
I can't and
it's agony.

For the Little Girl Growing up in G16

Circling Cinderella under corrugated plastic
Colours flash as you spin, dancing through
puddle water, rainbows, glitter on concrete

Laughter lilts between breezeblock:
osmosis of joy. I wonder what stories
you'll tell over beers in 15 years:

First time riding a bike down the Greenway?
The day you move away? Spotting yourself
in old photos, on dad's shoulders

on the day the bulldozers came?

Tilbury Town

Life line altered irrevocably by
tartan straps:
> 'Fix up ya lip!'

Mockery of prissery - piss-uppery
The difference between

butter and jam	vs	butter or jam
sliced cheese	vs	grated cheese
		on toast.

Toilet paper ever forwards in
warmth warmth cacophony.

> *Don't listen to me, I was bussed*
> *over from an identikid town five miles up*

Terraced houses wind like warrens
conjoined by concrete corridors.
Streaks of bare wood shine through
peeling red fences.
Back gate opens up
door swings open,
warmth pours out.

Do you know how often I think of you?
The radiance of your child's curls on social distract me
with what ifs. Our mothers were twins.

Six years ago I crossed the marshes
tearing my shoes to pieces, do you remember?
How I slipped in the mud, onto my back
arms reaching? I learned the value of a sturdy soul.

Wash Day

After Jericho Brown

I watch my washing machine trundle around,
spinning soap in, dashing dirt out, softening.

The water gathers sweat, swaps for soap.
On Saturdays my mother gathered with six siblings

the Magnificent Seven are marched upstairs
hands in the tub, competing

like shirt sleeves dancing under water, they jostle for space, laughing
over who can make the shukka-shukka sound

hooping air into fabric, freeing an ocean of disinfected foam
into collars and cuffs worn from a week at school, by all your brothers.

Hand-me-downs handled with care.
Seven pairs of hands, two washboards, shukka-soap, softening.

Together, for each other.
I watch my washing machine trundle around.

Gal Dem

Back a yard,
Hands smooth cocoa butter over leg.
Lightbulb refracts in the shaft of gold
dancing down your shin.

Prepped, you saunter in
sharp shock of pink, juicy fruit
flashing through pearly whites.

Chicken Shop box, suspended
Blue bag lit from within,
leaking oil and spices like
blessings, a bossting.

The sun anoints you, uplifts you
When prowling en masse, on road
hunters of opportunity;
The restless, wild youth.

Lucozade

I'm in the boy's room, wrapped in blankets
                shivering, nauseous
Nanny holds the cup to my lips:
garlic and ginger, sliced and boiled in hot water
but I would much rather have orange Lucozade.
Steam rises. I drink. I feel
tersely, firmly loved.

In Community

She pulls the shutter down,
spiky bleach blonde hair
brassy, bright as her earrings
Geometry reflected in the swirling Gucci G's of her matching
cream and black knitted cardigan and legging set.
Beaded velvet hats and coral necklaces winking, secured behind chainmail.

Across the road, he absent-mindedly sweeps the front of his cousin's
fruit and veg shop. Batting at the dust, one-handed
Scrolling with the other, smiling
inwardly, as music blares, mutes.

Welts rise in palms,
sending endless psalms
for this
shopping trip
to end.

Pride is not a good trait in a slave

Big Man Sam picks oranges, 1962, California.
Pickup truck rumbles lazily through bright, sharp-smelling fields.

He's in the back with the other Strong, Black Men.
Sam's back is as broad as his nose.

Overseer shouts "Quiet, boy!" over shoulder to boot.
Back and nose raise, a decision is made.

Wife, two kids back home.
Him na feel fe call "pitney".

Funeral Fit For a King

Hops howl behind glass
praying him back into existence:
his booming laugh
and crooked teeth

Every
Single
Car
In the
Carpark:
Covered in cans

Still lit cigarette ends
litter the floor
Hot pink lippie
freshly impressed
on a plastic shandy cup.
Stiletto lifting,
dirt shifting underfoot.

Children skip around
scattered traffic cones
laughing as sweetly as
when he would throw and catch them;
when he was the centre of the world.

Green Thumbs Run in my Family

plucking itchy calluses
from the root of thenar's eminence
carrots beans
small, bright, slugworn;
from my grandfather's perfect patch of lawn
and in Bim, mangoes pineapples guava sweet air.

tearing at skin permeable as moss
digging my thumbs in,
picking my palm
white flowers, gauzy: cotton
tobacco; sugar.
spitting bitter bitten nails
towards dirt:
they root on air.

80079 1958

Bespeckled, behatted Blacks
step off in Tilbury as ships dock:
Two t'ird class tickets please, sah.
Ford factory hulks like Hephaestus
smoke pouring from
his twenty upturned mouths
Spark of anvils
flashing red from within.

Smell of industry.
      of revolution.

Advance in diesel darkness
as the tracks switch underfoot
coal chuff
huff sweat
on-on-on!
Cocoa, coal nibs
coloured people
working-class whites on!

One switch
switched wrong
collision - head on.

Rubber dinghy
bumps
the unwalked pebble shore.
Upstream
sewers run off to the sea.

Spring Evening Hymn

very important programme to watch
just heard of it
Great British Sewing Bee
I'll make a curry,
she said.
Stay for an hour or a day or forever I said
in my head.
In fact I type   *Sounds good x*

Dogs bark, foxes yowl
taut as drumskin, I thrum in time

So-fires sparkle in her deep blue eyes
Sa-fires in the crease of her smile
So-fee-yahs in the crook of her arm
as Soph pulls her hair back
stirring curry in my kitchen
                in her socks.

Broke quarantine to lie apart,
to breathe the same air
and each soft exhale brings us
closer and closer
together.

Transmission

If this is just conversation, why can I feel the electro magnetic spark that powers your
heart from all the way over here?
You must be doing that on purpose. How else can I taste
the soft flicker
of your increased
heart
rate
on my tongue.

Our voices soft as though viral tendrils could
curl into sound waves
curl into birdsong and barks
curl around the soft gravel
crunch of a blush trainer
curl around your words and mine. Still
I lean in,
holding my breath
for your approach.

Shushed at each step by a waterfall of delicate green knife edges trickling between
my sandals' leather straps, we remain a stone's throw apart.
Knee high, ankle deep in grass your running dog brushes past my leg.
This second-hand contact
is exhilarating
nauseating
divine.

Crossed leg, solid thigh golden trail of sweat:
Ambrosia.
Lips part, impart a line that lies along the conch of my ear:
Benediction.

Patina of constellations on the mottled brick walls outside your orbit.
Tortoise shell cyclists zip forwards, back arched, peering between protection of
helmet and mask.
Fat red bricks uphold a white rabbit, pink nose glistening, sniffing at clouds
Graffiti lays it plain:
THIS IS THE END.

And then re a li ty fra c tu res in a diagonal shaft of light
as panic seeps through the presenter's practiced dulcet tones:
The news swaddles me juvenile.
Our dual screen duvet duet soothes
You're typing… Sheets rustle
An imaginary exhalation
on the nape
of my neck.

I flinch, asynchronous.
Where have you been? I just want to know, where were you over the past seven days?
Did you cough, or sneeze, is it suicide to slip between your open thighs as they rest,
innocently gathering gravel from the concrete curb?

Police trot past, their truncheons move as though twirling ribbons through honey,
slicing sparks.
We stand apart
dry-mouthed and panting.
From our 'walk and a chat' I was left
sweating, vibrating, bereft.

We use to go raving every weekend

               up!
fling ya arms
dramatic twist of the head   hah!
you stamp as
lights dazzle at crescendo
mouf twis up
making eye-contact with the DJ like
don't play me
           DROP THE TING NAH

It's that out of your head
feeling, me in my body
on a wave of song while
sweating in time to the beat, feeling.
It's not warm enough, dark enough, loud enough, packed enough in my living room and
flatmates don't bump and grind on their way to the fridge.
But my hunger is deep.

Character Flaw

Never bought a lighter in my life.
Slipped into pockets from
park benches, pub tables:
'Have you got a light?'
P---- sits on my bed,
ignores the horde,
ignores her fire, her flicker in my jar.
My face reflects off the curved class:
a thief caught holding the gold.
Nuts, isn't it? What a spread.
Dragonlike, I keep my eye on
mine and yours.

Dégustacion

Sweetwater sizzles under
Thunderdrum's clap

Drags her tongue
Across his double oxê

As he bites her ear,
Cups breast with palm

Fragrant hills rise from tundra
Welt-like, radiating warmth.

Call Me By Your Name

Sunbreak through cumulus, morning unfurls across treetops, crows perch on aerials, aligned. In these moments the type of SPF you have downstairs doesn't matter. Neither does the brand of your shoes, the colour of your chipped nail varnish as you finger your left earlobe, absent.

I can sense your distance. The inability to feel the softness I've wrapped around you. I'm still processing your face bent over a panting dog, the luxury of the deep scratch you offer his lower back, your laugh.

I promise I will hold this quiet, allow you freedom, movement, friendship over the gilded cage of passion. Thigh exposed in white cutoffs I promise I will hold this quiet exposed shadow of a breast allow freedom, movement, friendship over the gilded cage of passion.

Siri, play: Call Me By Your Name.

By Any Other Name

It's right there for her to see
in my email address and signature
yet she called me Dora, deleted it.
Constant misspelling, cloying sweetness…
Ten years ago, the CEO yells out: Lauren!
At what point do I become myself? How am I distinguished
from your memory of an ex-colleague,
the celebrity spelling, initialisation, anglicisation?

Shame burns through my face,
hot and sticky, obvious to anyone.
You've created this tension, this tip toe on tight rope
To you it's nothing, I'm as sweet as I am.
The anger is a thorned chord around my neck
I squeeze myself into extinction.

Incurable

After Dorothy Parker

Why walk when you can
run headlong into a field of
roses, dizzied by the perfume
the blooms, the delight of
newfound love.

Rose-tinted running when
you could walk, past
your traumas, bruises packed
off with your sense,
you darling fool.

It's raining and you're running
when you should walk, the
feels hit faster, the freshness
reminds you to breathe and
tomorrow you will have a cold.

Running when you should walk
Holding hands, arms swinging,
when you could walk, we run
again and again
into eros.

What a summer to be washed away

My undoing:

A Minnie Riperton record from
a woman wilder than sunflowers.

Sparrows perched fat as figs
on a cutting of rosemary.

Kisses as lifegiving as falling rain
from someone with dubious morals.

Eye-level with the oven, again
finding a new favourite recipe.

Breadcrumbing

Pigeons flock to you
Fresh as corn. Kisses so deep
sparks leave a shadow.

Crosslegged, intently staring at the wall, through which each trill of the neighbour's voice and music is amplified. A very specific ethnological experiment. Eyes closed it sounds like mum's house, where love came down - a man who only comes around at midnight, who only wants to see me when everything is outta sight.

Slowly, I extend my right arm, reaching out to pluck the night from their air. Pulling the night through breezeblock into open lap, dusting the night of cocaine, I cradle her close - a starlight look in our eyes. All this love that I've given and still when darkness falls I can't help the way I feel.

Transference

Luna was heavy that night
sending grey-green ripples out
across the algae-laden lock.
Calling out to us
as we turned our backs
to ascend the ladder.

Everything: milky
crystal white
spent gas canisters singing
smoked out buds
still crackling out illumination.
We watched our step.

Felt the tarmac tremble before
my Doc steps.
Purple light quartered in
a wall-sized window
(more than six) shifting shadows
in a supposed squat.

Uighur Lament

I

Sisters
Sisters
Sisters
1B black
Veiled in pinks and reds and golds!
Entwined in triplicate
Private art, hidden treasure
Outside, wrapped
When at home unfurled.

II

Sisters shorn
Journey: The razor travels
Hair by hair
As they weep, clumping
Tangling, downward - oh!
Line by line
The sisters fall
Beauteous, bountiful locks
Deep warm chestnut rain
Oh, how it rained.

III

At camp we learn the rules of citizenry
At camp, in each prayer
We kiss the feet of their
Glorious leader.
At camp they feed us sacrilege
At camp they eat our choice.

VI

March in step, we
March in step, we
Know right
From wrong.
March in step, we
March in step, we'll
Never
Go home.
Brother is lost
Sister lost worst.
Those that are left march in step.

What the Atlantic said, after capitalism

After Kathleen Jamie & Maya Angelou

I rise across the pebbles, slowly inching up my tides
I swell your plastic towards shore, I suckle at your tires.
I rise over abandoned boats, the loved ones lost to fires.
I rise across the channel, sinking schools and ending lives.
I drink the politician's brew of oil and gold and lies
And brewing in my stomach is the end we all surmised.

Float away sea navigators seeking more, seeking to thrive
Land a coral reef all splendour where the righteous all arrive
When the parliament has sunken and the pigs silence their cries
Softly sow yourself in Drexciya
Where you my love, will rise.

The First Time

Ever I heard,
That
Song
I was swaddled in towels, feet wrapped in sheets
on the way home from mum's salon.
Street lamps passed, swinging in lazy lullaby, all soft.
Between the chairs, your clattering wrist
moving with grace, controlled and calloused.
She was taking us home.
I stare out of the window,
remembering other lives, before the life lived in mine
erased them, pushing them backwards
into the dark.

Universal

Afternoon sun reflects off the
crack-screen totem I cradle.

Lyricless music holy and clear ripples
in my wait for benefaction.

Guy on the other end asks me,
asks if we have   any   source of income?

Palms open, cheeks hot with sorrow
and with need

and left without.

Red Flag

Flatmate begs down phone:
"Watch me take K and chainsmoke?"
Our door is left ajar.

Howl

There are nights when I am streets deep
in the memory of your gaudy purple laugh. It
pulls me into mischief
out the window out of bed
into the starlight glinting from your crooked grin.
I want to dive in.

There are nights when I explode awake, a
mass of curls erupting from my mouth, a
shapely thigh, muscles tense and twitching
presses against my gore from inside.
How you fill me with delight.

Botany Lessons

For T

Imagine:
A small, bright seed folded in
Deep warm darkness sending
Ripples of energy pulsating
Potential, aware, shuddering
At the slightest brush
Pulling back into the
Space where
Nirvana
hides.

Imagine:
Root system
Branch of branch
Subatomic sensation
Nerve endings endlessly
Seeking oasis in every drop
Until nadir becomes climax.

Wind whistles around the mountain range at the centre of the earth. There we stand, barefoot in the ice, lip reading by millimetre. There we stand, on the knife edge of life and death, entwined.

Gossamer Emotion

Giving myself a lesbian manicure, cut so close the pith
is on show. I wonder what everyone else is doing
with theirs. The white detritus crawling along the underside of
the nail, suddenly and bashfully unveiled. What does everyone do
with the moss that creeps out from under closed eyelids
and out from open mouths at the most inopportune moments?
When making eye contact with a new lover, perhaps, or
while trying to sleep at night? What does everyone do
with theirs? I've tried cutting it off, but your memory
clings to the bed of my skin; I am exposed.

Funeral Rites

Unceremonious chatter
from parrots on the vine
belies the solemnity of the occasion

Leering, jeering between stone fruit
left to rot in salt air
left to drop in the gash in the terminal green.

You peer down
Pitter patter earth clatter
on the roof

You peer into
the heart of the wound -

      And that's when they grab you

Heel-toe peeled up
Slung like a spud sack
Knees across elbows

World inverted

      And that's when you take flight.

Nurishment

After Warsan Shire

Why don't you get Nurished? Try our nutritionally enriched milk drink,
Blast caverns into canyons in the search for iron ore

with its creamy caramel taste, fortified with vitamins and mineral,
I scale the dunes of your cheeks, hack through fields to find

good source of protein, and comes in four delicious flavours
freshwater. In mind's eye, bare toes dig in sand on shore.

The friendly not that says, "we see you". The warm hug that
When open, mudcracks shiver brightly through desiccated clay

says "we're with you". A pat ont he back that says "well done you!"
and I am alone, one pocket filled with fool's gold – I pour it on the floor.

Whether you're on the go, or just looking for a deliciously creamy, tasty treat,
Why don't you eat something?

Nurishment is here for you.
Fractures so deep take millennia to restore.

You Can't Sleep Here, Love

Cream carpet
as far as the eye can see
under the bed

Lost shoes, dumb belles
That sinking feeling
comes in waves

Song regains tune
Click tocks
Screaming stops

Love, I'm sorry but you can't sleep here.

The War to End All Wars

disassociation
is a very fine thing
i float, un em bodied
through factions waving placards
robed in blood
      in earth
      in bile.

heaven's fallen seraphim
bellow at the full passing clouds
obscuring them from
god's languorous gaze:
                "Black Lives Matter!"
cries echo over
palatial marble rooftops:
                "Black Lives Matter!"

a black dog
roves before me
sniffing and snipping through
rustling
flapping
and nascent wingtips alike.
beautiful, hopeful youth
fists clenched, wide-eyed,
calling for the Revolution:
                "Black Lives Matter!"
eddies of dust swirl
between the horses' hooves:
                "Black Lives Matter!"

i try to find my stillness
                No Justice, No Peace
i lead a call, i falter
                No Justice, No Peace
i practice my self-soothing
                No Justice, No Peace

i'm not sure i believe you

No Justice, No Peace
No Justice, No Peace
No Justice, No Peace

no end.

Second Date (With a Pisces)

She turns to me, enchanted,
bubbles escaping up to ether

But it's clear she wouldn't last on land

Her lazuli coat is unseasonable
The lace of her shoes, too tight

Still I tilt my silver water catcher
Invite her to lie in my meagre mirror

When it whispered in strain, I retreated
Unwilling to wait for the crack.

He Remembers with a Smile...

He told me: 'Be kind to yourself.' I'd almost forgotten how we'd clung to each other, how I could feel his heart pounding against mine. How the hug lasts slightly too long, how tentatively we pull away. He remembers with a smile things that bring me shame.

It is very difficult to tell someone you love to stop seeing someone they love. Uniquely difficult to put your feelings first, at least for certain types of people.

I've always been a cynic, but I've tried to do the right thing. Difficult. To see him sat across the living room, legs crossed. Interesting. A chance to read the situation without judgement. The sensation of being outside again.

Accepting that I've chosen how it goes, how and where to connect and with whom adds calm, some hope.

Feeling difficult to sit in my blessings without guilt. A lack of compassion. I find it too much, maybe everyone else does too.

Time to think is so fucking precious.

Timid Heart

Through thorns and
auburn berries left to
wizen on the vine

light trembles
Altar-warm
a cathedral window:

light calls.
Panic in the black of every beat.
Can you hear me? Rustling

up the hill can you feel me
block the wind?
Soft as mothdust

I settle and bask
in your glorious flame.

Rain Again

I tried to soothe away
the staccato of your knees
by nestling, penguinlike to
combine my heat with yours.

You smoothed the waterproof
between myself and the wind
face raised, unflinching.
When you wished it would rain again

a hidden gate in the wall swung open
inviting you to come home.

this, but harder

it's hard to keep up, like
tidal.
like, a river
rushing between my breasts
like

your hands around my neck
looking
into my eyes with that
blankness
we both know will
never
shift

mouthing me your want

*What was said **what was heard***

can i come to your **bad things in the past ?**
when i saw i'm **so many of my friends**
i thought: 'why not?'

queer and vulnerable in the group chat
posting about how hot i look addicted to heroin.
mixing benzos and opiates in the psych ward.

i've lost friends
on the same drugs
i OD'd on.

Intuition

I'd been hurt: *"Putting his wants ahead of yours?"*
I was sobbing and...
Maybe I don't want something more traditional.

We took acid together, they held me.
Discussed narcissism in action
the lows, the lies, the shame.

They told me I am loved, I am enough,
text me something really lovely.

I can see this being a big problem.

Like Church

Your marble monument shines
from the heart of Darkness. I trace
the etchings of your facade,
dig fingers into pits caused by erosion
and in this way dare dream
myself
one step closer to god.

earnest

feel him still as
i bring paper to
eye-level, fingers
rustling softly against
rizla kingskin
before my tongue tip
flicks out to lick
i spit: "What?"

he opens his mouth
arms steepled, earnest-eyed
under soft yellow lamp-light.
folded peaches of his hands
pressing in prayer
> *(lord, please let the right words form)*
> *(lord, carry the breeze escaping my lips in tune)*

this bleach blonde
english rose
baby pink punk
he says:

At the Strikers

You're just out of grasp
Facial features fragmenting into blur
as you roll past.
Figment of my adoration
close yet far as constellation.
I swear, I saw you at The Nelson.

Are you coming?   *Do you fancy a drink?*
Do you remember? Do you understand?
                                Didn't we meet before?

Lean up in the garden, eyes
raise to graffiti, streetlamps chiselling
cheekbones
Near and so far.
I swear I saw you at The Nelson
sleeve dipped in pub slick
Boisterous, laughing with the bar staff.
Even when you tip the tip cup up
no one bothers to make a fuss.

Do you remember? Do you understand?
We met before?   *you held my hand?*

You're blurred under pink awning
Boot pressing a fag to the dirt,
the flare catches on green
eyeshadow, hazel eyes almost close

against the smoke, against the light.
But I swear I saw you slipping
to the toilet for a bag?
Swaying, pondering the paintings
Your ghost dances hot and lithe round
every concrete column, circling me
like you did, dazzling me
like you did, and

Didn't we hold hands? Do you remember?
Do you understand?

By the time I gather strength to ask
the moment's gone, your shade has passed.

Little One

I dreamed the weight of our child in my gut. She presses heavy on my bladder from inside, I feel the crushing softness weigh on my arms and the strength that rises to meet it.
I feel phantom fragility in the warm and heavy head that rests on my chest, my body aflame with the power to protect.

Sweet smell of milk, caramel syrup rises from the crease of her left knee.

I had concerns. I worried she could have turned to brittle under him, that she could snap. I had concerns about her, soft and fine as muscovado, freckled face resting in the crook of my arm as her body shakes out his small slights and her teeth rattle to rid herself of judgment.

She could be whatever he wanted.

She sits on the floor, cross-legged as I sat cross-legged between my mother's knees, as my mother sat between her mother's knees. I divide her afro hair into sections and smooth them with coconut oil: 'Daddy loves you, sweetpea. Daddy tries his best sugarplum. Daddy shows he loves you in lots of little ways, you just have to look real close.'

She could be whatever he wanted.

Hair wraps around itself as my fingers click in thoughtless rhythm: 'Daddy didn't mean it. 'Daddy didn't mean to slam the door. Daddy didn't mean to say bad words.'

He cried as he drove me away from the home we had tried to make: 'You would have made such a good mum.' His hands shake the wheel, we veer dangerously into the next lane. For a second, I think: 'I always knew that he would be the death of me.'

When the door shuts I kneel before my mother. She reaches one calloused hand towards my forehead as I close my eyes to shake out his small slights. My teeth rattle to rid myself of his judgment.

Little one, on days like this each passing second carries the sorrow and the joy of your unbeing.

Part 2

Rupture

We lay together in liminal space, in utter disgrace
unable to leave the zone of discomfort
to contort ourselves beyond projection
Anonymous and lonely, unproductive and alive

How can you tell photoshop from fate?
When the mouth moves so convincingly

When the mouth movements are so convincingly aligned, it's deep
They make you say whatever they want.
Make you say: *More, more, more*
Make you say: *My discomfort is illusion*
and rest is for the weak.

You've been here before
so kick the brick from out your lip
Kick misguided faith in the all powerful 'L'
train to non-place, to hyperdrive
through overheated junkspace
Formless, shapeless, endless

You, half empty, again. Left between everyone and no one,
like tipped chair on stained carpet, like a window left ajar
Anonymous and lonely, unproductive and alive
Again
The imprint of your intervention lay eerie on my breast

Again
Again
Again
Again
Again

Disassociating?

Reader may loop until satisfied they exist.

am i fine?
i   am.
   am   i?
      i...

      fine!
i am...
i...
  am fine?

     i...
  am   i.
    i   am?
    i'm   fine.

Three Months

everything stopped for
three months or so
                        no news.
cbt, every day, meditation
trapped with the other nuts repeating
                                repeating behaviours.
got in the car, mum
held my hand
            the radio
            the news.

so many died
numbers spin into dots
out the window, we pass shops
                            shops are shut.
three months or so looking in
                                in rehab
'social distancing'?
                        shops are shut.

they stood on his neck
like Eric Garner

                            repeating
                            repeating behaviours

everything stopped

the little black dots

                            so many died!
            so many died!

it could have been me
                        please
turn the radio
        the news, off
                        please
i can't breathe

        no news.

Matter of Britain

Regarding Excalibur Estate, Catford

Robin, stunned
Out of night out of tree out of sky

(casualty of war)

Hot air churns clods of the foundation,
roots reach upwards, roaring with fire.
Homes turn to ash,as
undersoil becomes top.

Prisoners of war heft rocks
mix concrete, raise beams, turn gravel
muttering about *Tedeschi bastardi*
turning gravel, raising beams, sandwiching poison
between plasterboard, sour-mouthed.
When the apple tree sings at night
across the slanted roof,
it almost sounds like home.

How dreary, deary me,
she sniffs

He hops up the grey concrete ramp
Flings his sticks to the side, says:

Come on Maude,
You ain't never seen a posh tub like that'n!

Kisses the false pout until it gleams
A ray of light tiptoes across
white sheets in late morning
Warm skin. She holds her smile in ember.
He knows it's there.

When I arrived, the house was already dust
Birdsong and constant breeze
echoed through single pane windows
Spiders eyed me sympathetically
from asbestos-filled gaps
between ceiling boards.
Whipped with solitude and sorrow
I clung to the chipped wooden floor.

Over time, overturned soil
reveals the truth.
Creatures chitter over a small metal airplane
engraved with earth, unclaimed.
Brambles crack concrete slabs
Shovel leans on shabby shed, at its root:
Half a Hindi CD, a child's plastic toy.
I kneel, reading the stories of the earth
Nailbeds in the flowerbed,
sorting for Avalon.

Storm Warning

I sit in the chasm
between need and want
burning for you, M-.

I've been looking for you
in Craigslist ads
from lonely men;
In chatrooms, comment boxes.
I looked for you in the
yes-yes-no of Tinder swipes
You were nowhere to be found.

I looked under her tongue,
thought I found you but
she left and so
you left, too.

Looked for you
round the corner from
my cousin's house;
In the tangy lid sip
of vodka from Nan's drinks cabinet;
Behind graffiti spattered bins;

I saw your eyes shine out
of C---'s mad blues;
Sparking danger under the hood of a car;
In the long grass of the park;
In bleach.

I watched you spill
and I ran to you:
Face down on the
living room floor I'd
run, run, run
to you, M-.

Why can't you
find me?

Swinging

Light cascades across splintered floorboards
A bare bulb, set swinging
by the breeze of the front door.

The rude glare surprises him,
he who did not want to make a fuss.

Miami Beach

After Jericho Brown

Fold ground leaves into paper, turn on angle, press together.
A ring of foam surrounds me, lifting me into salt water
Without ego, the pressing weight of supremacy on my throat
Burst of sweetness, teeth sink through the skin of a mango handed to me by a mother.

A ring of foam surrounds me, lifting me into salt water.
Upturned nose, eyes widened with disdain, apprehension, judgement
Burst of sweetness, teeth sink through the skin of a mango handed to me by a mother
I draw my line in the sand, heart aflame and hands shaking.

Upturned nose, eyes widened with disdain, apprehension, judgement.
The tide pulls me close, the salt draws out pain.
I draw my line in the sand, heart aflame and hands shaking.
Who would you be without the pain, she asks? How would you stand?

The tide pulls me close, the salt draws out pain,
Burst of sweetness, teeth sink through the skin of a mango handed to me by a mother
Who would you be without the pain, she asks? How would you stand?
I fold ground leaves into paper, turn on angle, press together.

Animals

I

feet padding heartpounding
through jungletangle
blind fear fist pulls hair he
laughs hefucking LAUGHS
wet grass andthe
grating biting
un-human:
djinn or bitter petty god
red and raised
twitching drooling

Mine, he said. Mine.

II

Sent up the mountain at first blood
Wilting, shitting, sore.
Pale pebbles chip at my feet
Empty handed bare shouldered
Illuminated by a thankless moon.

Scent of fresh pine winds up the path
Soothes my headache -
Balm for flushed cheeks
Red hot aching breasts

At apex,
When Mother blesses me,
Warm rain washes blood from my ankles, my feet.

I return reborn.

Rid yourself of body hair

And walk on broken needles
double bass thrum of tendon, poised to stumble
Exposed snail shells balance on salt
on pebbles, on gratings, ever slower
as the shaker lopes behind. Unzipping unsettling,
unspanxing an ache as all settles
into the wrong place. Compress
your groaning softness to hot nausea grimace. Do I look pretty now?

Thank you for revealing the final boundary between yourself and the world.
for showing us where you might bleed, where we might bite.
For shivering under stars on shards, sight serrated,
udders unveiled for hop-breath to suckle.

Cousins

Your t-shirt hair flicks just as well as Ariel's
and I want to be part of your world.
Our totem pole laughs as you dance lithely.
I'd always been taller
until I wasn't.

Flat backed and invisible
against a pale yellow sheet
my body was consumed by fire
which both cleansed and erased me
yet in his eyes, you were hell.

We sit on a park bench to
watch our paired demons pass.
You and me, starved and swollen
and I love you so much
that I can't hear what you're telling me.

Continual Unthinking Terrorism

I

He looked me in the eye and said:

> *Sometimes*
> *You want*   *sirloin steak*

> *And sometimes*
> *You want*   *McDonalds*

Nodding towards the plump blush-brunette
enthusiastically spilling out of the box he'd placed in the corner
Reducing me   and her   and us

To: seared   animal   sandwich
Consumable   digestible   excretable
empty   calories   protein
Iron   flesh

His teeth glinting, because
Surely a woman-lover must know

All women are prey.

II

Diesel rises from his pits. He towers over you. You are violently aware of your still wet breasts, loose beneath plum towelling.

Why can't you just do it the way I want?

You chance a look up at him. Beads of sweat, framed by his backwards baseball cap, refract the familiar blank stare of an ex-lover who once threw your clothes into the street. You are aware of your pubic hair rustling against your dressing gown as you shift to veil your thighs.

You already learned that when you have angered a predator, sometimes it's best to remain still.

Be still, and when it's safe - run.

III

'I knew before I went up there'

Scraped knees, high heels
Stumbled up the greenway
'No' zipped into her leather jacket.

At some point between the
Steps and the benches,
He took it (back).

IV

unstoppable force, immovable object

Rocks make moves
Over millennia
Stretching pressing breathing
Baked by sun
Fractures form
For flexible rigidity
Water foams
Swirls and stills
To sand

The woman you always thought I could be,
Yet never waited to meet:
Potential personified

Care as casket.

A Field Guide to Getting Lost

At horizon, inhale
Towards an open window
And if the sun calls you,
Accept.

At exit, inspect the earth
For passing insects,
Welcome them by name and
Move.

At corner, allow the breeze
To tease your unwashed hair
Use your hands to follow
Suit.

At exhale, angels whisper
Under oak. Each leaf calls you
Lost. Each leaf calls you
Home.

Hunger

We embrace in the kitchen
ribs sticky with jealousy

of your solidity, gravity, heft
My birdlike collarbone,
hollow waist, invisible wrists

How could you know?
How could you know?

I've been aching to be fed.

Solo Canto

1

Hands swing in pairs
One pair, unpaired. Hers.
She turns them over, stares.
Stamps them unknowable,
Infinitely impaired.

2

Her hair: floral, florid. She vibrates
Glitter-eyed across planes of existence.
Do you know the Golden People?
He creaks, pupils deep as grief.
She rebukes him, laughing.

3

She cups his face as they circle,
Delivering a serenade for sore eyes
She is blind to his hands,
Hanging loose at his sides.

4

Inhale, exhale: chaturanga
Sweat pearldrops into open mouth
Oceanic flare of salt
Where stillness and movement align.

Manic Pixie Dream Wife: Postscript

Sometimes, when I'm walking to the station
or at the corner shop,
I see the flash of someone your height:
Shaved head
Soviet brow
Masked.

I blanche, wonder if you'd dare be in my town
Imagine you
frowning down a snow-covered street
typing furiously at a cafe
Never seeing me at all.
In-jokes and playfights seep through the

you-shaped gash in the world
rendered meaningless after your last flight.

It's not to say that I miss you, exactly.
It's just hard to pretend it never happened.

Little big you, nestled in the crook of my arm
adoring-eyed, champion cheerleader

Never quite saw past the glitter
and when you did

you fled.

An Aviary of Common Birds

The weight of the clouds
peeking under the blinds
were too much to bear:
A lullaby of loneliness
on a magpie's wing.
At the street corner crows
taunt me, peck at my hair.

Called in sick, again.

Escape Escape Escape Still

I escape to the garden, when my room traps me.

I escape to the benches, wet concrete and the reassuring rustle of nettles.

I escape to the broken tiles and flickering streetlamps the overhanging chatter from richer people's dwellings the clatter of machinery and the passing of postmen to remind me I live that time passes and I am part of the world when I need to escape the mirror.

All is still inside the mirror.

Shame hangs leaden on your limbs, weight lolls your head against a breast bruised with disgust.

All is still inside the mirror.

I escape - roll full bodied off a cliff, land heavy and bloodied, wind through a valley all to feel the sun on my face.

I escape - into movement, past entire worlds whirlwinding past in confusion, their kicked up dust reminding me that I was.

That I am.

Alive.

I escape to the garden, when the house becomes too much.

I escape to the solitary green plastic chair on bewjewelled concrete, beaten as it is by roots and weeds.

I escape to the chair when the house begins to collapse on me when the unboxed wedding presents wail from our spare room, escape to squirrels stealing from the birdfeeder watch them tiptoe acrobatically across the plastic washing line framing futile attempts to unearth an overgrown patio - for BBQs that never happened - escape to the robins and parakeets and the watchful gaze of crows when I need to escape the house.

All is still inside the house.

I knelt when crawling across the sofa hadn't moved you. When presents and presence hadn't moved you, the house was still. Still, I waited there, eyed you on the sofa, statuesque, adorned you and then went out.

But god, what an ache.

All was still, and the echoes vibrate through my body now, of absence, of loss: a small girl sweeping glass under adults, invisible and untouched, still.

Repair

After 'The Fountain' by Alexandrina Hemsley & Yewande 103

What do rib cages and spines know?

Grey areas are not a flaw
but part of the design.
Returning to intimacy

after harm. Plug hole,
sink hole
collapse.

Accepting uncertainty
in the imprint when the mouth
moves like a tipped chair, like

a stained window, like a jar.
To be fluid is messy
some structures respond as if

you need to clean yourself up.

We don't want to share our spillages,
we want to be dry, **not in need**
of each other. (See figure 4.)

How tentatively we pull away.

Spaces that make my mouth
dry and language fail. Sensation
of being outside again

insisting my reality is real.

Mirrors

When I couldn't see my reflection on the tube as a kid,
I'd render myself invisible
hands on knees,
pressing into the
  scratchy seat beneath
eyes reverential, confined within my frame.
Weighing the firm solidity of thighs s p r e a d i n g in jeans
Each individual cream stitch
both pulling and pushing
like clenched, bared teeth.

Up: Each face delicately angled away.
Bodies shifting,   breathing,
one-armed swinging, thumbing at glass, immersed in
solo lullaby.
Patent leathers point away. In shuffling buckles I spy
wild-eyed and golden
Medusa.

Anyway,
we don't ride the tube any more.

We sit unreflected, entombed in silence; or
submerged in the drip-
of other people's sound.
I seep half-in   half-out
one arm down the wrong hole
spinning webs to hang on mirrorless walls
in wait
for the coming of Spring.

Tiny Deaths and Resurrections
(For PRISM)

heart stuck
       i open my mouth

                                    unsure what will come out

waterfall of ants
sodden, sorry string of paper dolls

lips stretching
       toad emerging, protesting
uprooting me as rock

eyes black-black, flat
reborn in the
stubborn tilt of a lip
        chin
           eyebrow
              shoulder

these childish protestations

how else to say: me - here
      you -   there

Tonight I can write the saddest lines

After Pablo Neruda

Tonight I can write the saddest lines
Write for example: 'The stones in my stomach shift when I walk.'

The wasps in my heart search for sweetness and bitter abyss. They'll only find one.

Tonight I can write the saddest lines.
I fell down the stairs so neatly that no one heard.

My mouth is a dripping sieve --
Wait.
      a fortress, gate clattering open shut open shut, customless

The well is covered in lichen.
No one is coming.

Decree Absolute

Heart lurches when a moon-eyed couple walk my way
I duck into an alley
clutching my pearls
        my breast
        my cunt:
smothering that wailing siren call

No good ever comes from her want
but she wants, she wants.

You flooded the drought two days in a row - furiously focused, averted eyes. Held me
down by my neck as I willingly opened my parched mouth, revealing the desperation
hiding at the base of my dry clicking throat, swollen tongue and tonsils undulating
with need. Mouth pinched to a kiss by columns of stone, I gasped please please more
more more until dambust stars sparked at the confines of my cage. Something broke.

I wanted to drown, you helped.

I almost died the last time I fell in love.

Last time I fell in love
I haunted the walls
I'd build to house him

See me now? My strong legs, my quick chipped smile?
How could I let anyone
love me away?

SB: Why did you marry him?

We were art.
Some questions have no answers
can't be answered (yet)

No good has ever come from
it, from the search for it, from
the offering ofit, from
thetaking ofit, the
givingitfromitfromIT
No good comes from our want
but we want, we want.

And yet on some nights

The air is still close
with the scent of him
pressed along my spine like exoskeleton
breathing into the small hairs curling at the nape of my neck
the arch of his rib cage gently folding open, flowerlike.
Eyelashes brush skin
I drink deep.

Bloom

I was a seed nestled in the mycorrhizal soup, sped on by passing electrons when the great spark of humanity rapped my shell,
shook me apart until I was no more.

Myth and reason myth and truth
Creation myth opening finally
                    vividly.

Originally, at the start that is, I'd looked out at the expanse of nothingness, sighing.
Grew up in a normal house, angels posted at the foot of the stairs. They watched small acts of love, counted shards of glass until I couldn't fit the rooms any longer
left arm pushing out the front window
shouldering the ceiling above the TV

Next to which, there is a photograph of me with windswept hair, mid flight grimacing bright and terrified and
                    trapped and mad.

There is no photograph of the smell of fritters, the croon of the hot pan, the washing machine's soft rocking to let you know
that you are loved.

I remember the glow of the computer monitor (deep blue night blue) permeating my retina as I research the meaning of love and the
definition of beauty and the philosophies of sex and connection. They tell me I was fucking great on Myspace. They tell me I'm a ray of light the whistling sound of the moon the shadow
on the sun.

In the beginning there was a seed nestled, sleeping in the mycorrhizal soup
Snapped awake by passing electrons
Cracked by pressure, finally
            Beginning, vividly
                    Alive.

GROWING PAINS

Beware the insidious seduction of memory:
Winding round the neck,
Petrifying the face;
An ivy chain, coiling
Round the soft apricot pit
Between collar bones
Where breath, and hope seep in.
Sometimes you will wake in the night,
Wailing sodden
Fresh dream crusted
In the corner of each eye;
As you draw breath to howl
Seeds take root, and with these shoots
Life begins anew
Sore as a broken window
As the pale, raw flesh
Of a knee skinned,
You begin again
Roots lengthen into the abyss,
Fat purple figs swell from heavy branches.
      Look forward.
  Look up.
Take a bite.

'How are You?'

I'd forgotten who I am:
Call it cause or symptom but
I'd forgotten how to talk:
The pieces were to hand
but un   p e a c e   able,
all I had were bleating noises, the
rssrssstttsss of pink noise
I'd forgotten that my tongue moves,
that my throat ripples
with laughter sometimes.

Depression is so tricky, so endless:
The black hole you've always lived in;
You who have never been loved and will
never be forgiven, breaker of hearts
and friendships and marriages; acidic,
venomous unsafe one, the snake
endlessly eating itself, coiled
inwards, spiralling, hysterical.
Mad.

But yeah, no, I'm alright now I think
Sometimes I feel so nauseous I have to
lie down and I find myself staring into the
distance and not quite finishing sentences
but

Sleep–

Love is not obsession.

Love is not a brown curl falling on a wide shoulder.

Love is not the waiting. Love is not the wait.

Love is not the warmth in your gut when you feel them looking at you from across the room.

Love is not control, nor is it controlling.

Love is not the smashing of glass. It is not a fist through a wall, no matter how hard they try to convince you.

Love is not isolation.

It is not the pull in the middle of the night, nor is it waking with tears in your eyes, clutching their memory to your maw.

Love is not endorphins, the flood and the rush.

Love is not us against them, 'you wouldn't do that if you loved me'.

Love is not sleepwalking, nor is it sleep.

I won't ask you to taste me on your lips, nor to feel the manna from my desperate phone call in the dark.

I won't ask you to wake with my smile on your brow, nor to want to hold me when the moon is high and wild.

I won't ask you to want me over muesli, nor to press your morning mouth to mine.

I won't ask you to wonder where I go in dreams, nor to wonder how ours can blossom and entwine.

I can't ask for your laughter when I'm silly, nor your forgiveness when I fail.

I can't ask you to hear me through the fog of my misadventures, nor to see me through the glamour.

I won't ask you to apologise.

I won't ask you to stay.

I can't ask you to stay.

I can't ask.

I won't ask.

It's not love.

Angel

The ascension of a dust mote carries great
consequence to the world around it. Particles
shift, things never remain the same.

Intuition, inner strength multiplied by 0

01: 01
Fight for the happiness of your inner child
beloved one. Know that

your thoughts become your reality

   1 . 1 1 p m
"Good thoughts put forth good seeds
Bullshit thoughts rot your meat."

Remember, the celestial army has got your back.

       0 2 : 0 2   Cross palms with joy
when she passes, life is too short to worry
about things you can't control.

Good turns to bad, bad turns to good.

   = 2 . 2 2 2
Take heart, keep faith
    keep moving, keep balance

Continue up the path

        £ 777 . 77
of wisdom and you shall reap
        great rewards.

Apex

Black woman, apex
Thighs and mind of thunder
Grounded, solid

Catches me in her stratospheric eyeline
in the future sight of higher love.

The mountainous everything of her
so bright I can barely behold.

I hide in the shade of her lashes
Awe-struck, knee-fallen, parched
Reflected in salt water

The mountainous everything of her -
of us - so bright I can barely behold.

Museum of Indelible Auras

After Lucille Clifton

For so long they passed through my corridors, never meeting;
Feet treading dirt into rugs meant to invite.
My kitchen buzzes with the sweet and bitter herbal taste of Mauby.
Noses wrinkle; my tongue torn out from their distaste
Demons writhe deep in my discoloured carpet,
wings synchronised to swim through sorrow like starlings on air.
A few membranes of memory whisper from the basement, where my sadness is
serene-wrapped, stacked on top of the wedding dress, the screams boxed.

After so many ascensions, still
Birds nest in the attic, the warm flurry of community
After so many ascensions, still
sweetness sticks to the roof of my mouth
After so many ascensions, still
not dead.

Chaos Theory

Everything hurts in the chasm
Each reach for help harms,
your tongue is a wasp
biting at sugar.

Everything hurts in the chasm.
Situationships shift clear as kaleidoscope
Your eye is an anchor,
dragging to depths.

Everything hurts in the chasm.
The pain of pebbles attests to
granite beneath. Your skin whispers
of salt wind

perhaps nearby, a shore.

Learning to be Afraid

of our mothers milk, of the potential
of nourishment, of healing, of new. Learning
to be afraid of the orange blossom
bloom of sparks at our sacrum,
of laughter across fresh sheets.

When we're loved it lifts
like a bell, rushing our heart like
a swooping bird, the crackle of autumn
fresh in our hair
despite the endless promise of dark. Love
is the offer to recline and to be embraced, yet
we jolt upwards like a child resisting sleep.
Hope will thaw you, if you let it.

We are afraid love will vanish.
When we are loved, we are afraid.

-wake

Coffee
Morning after
An open window, last night's
rain still stains the pavements
Closing the blinds against the builders
outside, the rumble of roadworks and people
Your face soft against my pillow,
our hair entangled
Shadowed sheets

You're going to be late for work babe. Again. And you're actually closer from mine.

Black silicone absurd against monstera
And wonderful you
The quiet in your absence more sweet for your presence
The wonder of waiting
Last night

Last night the words we could not say
bubbled on our tongues
On our lips, between us
Two seas kiss, an ocean apart
And you, with your bright heart
And the words
I cannot say.

Divine Order

Sudden change
of shower temperature as you consider
pulling a sickie

Eyes meeting in a crowded club,
lip corners curling with a
silent shared joke.

A doggy bag
from a passerby's pocket
in a moment of real need

Thumb hovering
to 'Call' your best friend, and
'answering' the phone instead

Waking from a sweat-drenched
nightmare, to a missed call
from mum.

Held breath
before lips touch
for the first time

Putting away your lighter,
coughing, after five attempts
to light a fag. Burning

A bundle of sage, lips
Pursed while your flatmate asks:
'Wait, are you trying to get rid of me?'

Sailing through green light
after green light, making the train
with two minutes to spare

Knowing not to walk your dog
at the quarry tonight,
even though... A crow

at the window, head tilted,
searching for you
when you could not find yourself

Sparklers fizzing in the press
of a bicep against yours,
as you smile towards the stage

A scarf taken by the wind, mourned,
and returned weeks later - sodden,
still loved - on the curb by your front door

Opening the back door
to let yesterday out
and the window to let today in.

Acknowledgments

Thank you to my parents Aletha and Roger, who gave me music, the moon and the night. Thank you to Orlando, for the books, for everything. To Paris and Kamarah, my darlings, I hope you know the world is yours.

Shout out to Christina Fonthes who hyped me up when I didn't even know I was a writer, and to Apples and Snakes for the opportunities to learn in a role flexible enough to write around - I'm so grateful. And especially to Owen Craven-Griffiths, for taking the time to read my early manuscript and being so confident in me when I'm flailing. Thank you to the sibstren - PRISM writers and Rewrite for your support and inspiration! Writing and sharing with Black women and Brown womxn and non-binary people of a range of ages opened my heart in ways I didn't know were possible.

With special thanks to Jah-Mir Early, Desree, the Repeat Beat Poet, Stephie Ronget Devred and to Theophina Gabriel, who first published me in Onyx Magazine (Liberation/Growing Pains). Thanks to SHE Magazine ('How are You?'), Ink, Sweat and Tears (Apex, Dasheen, How to Pronounce Dagenham), Marble Poetry Magazine (Green Thumbs Run in my Family), ANTHEMS Podcast ('Lust' - Transmission), Tamara Al-Mashouk and team behind Performance as Protest (War to End All Wars) and also for the stages I've been invited to share on.

Thank you to my friends for putting up with silence alternated with poetry spam - I'm sorry, I love you, I can't promise I'll change - but let's close this chapter together, yeah? Dinner at mine?

Big love to the Hackney Wick warehouse community and to the stall holders in Dalston and Deptford Markets.

LAY OUT YOUR UNREST